the
disregarded child
My Life with Autism

Tia Marie
Enjoy!

En Marie
EN24y

tia marie

the
disregarded child
My Life with Autism

TATE PUBLISHING & Enterprises

This book is designed to provide accurate and authoritative information with regard to the subject matter covered. This information is given with the understanding that neither the author nor Tate Publishing, LLC is engaged in rendering legal, professional advice. Since the details of your situation are fact dependent, you should additionally seek the services of a competent professional.

The opinions expressed by the author are not necessarily those of Tate Publishing, LLC.

Published by Tate Publishing & Enterprises, LLC
127 E. Trade Center Terrace | Mustang, Oklahoma 73064 USA
1.888.361.9473 | www.tatepublishing.com

Tate Publishing is committed to excellence in the publishing industry. The company reflects the philosophy established by the founders, based on Psalm 68:11,
"The Lord gave the word and great was the company of those who published it."

Book design copyright © 2010 by Tate Publishing, LLC. All rights reserved.
Cover design by Leah LeFlore
Interior design by Stefanie Rane

Published in the United States of America

ISBN: 978-1-61739-338-9
1. Biography & Autobiography, Personal Memoirs
2. Psychology, Psychopathology, Autism Spectrum Disorders
10.12.03

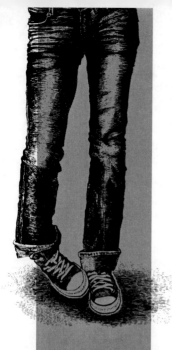

I am a twenty one year old girl with a mental disability called Autism. Autism ranges from a variety of types. I am a highly-functioning autistic person; which means that I'm able to think a little more like an average person, yet my brain functions very differently than most people. An example would be, I can talk and make simple decisions for myself; while low-functioning autistic people can't do those things. Autism is a social and learning disorder. I act in certain ways that others consider "strange," but I think they're normal behaviors. Until I learn that average people don't necessarily understand me unless I conform to the way they act. For those of you who have closed minds, the word "autistic" doesn't mean that the person is *stupid, retarded, crazy,*

Introduction

or any other insults you can throw at us. It just means that we need a little extra help than everybody else. In fact, a lot of autistic people are more intelligent and talented than some people think. Autistic people often get stereotyped but, like all other people, we are human beings with feelings and should be treated as such. We just have unique ways of expressing ourselves.

I have learned a lot about life over the years. There are times when I feel completely at ease and perfectly aware of what's going on around me. There are also times when I feel lost and upset. Unfortunately, many days were highly stressful for me in school. I go days and nights worrying about things happening that I don't like. For instance, I have trouble ignoring people who are mean to me. My family members and friends have to constantly remind me to go on with my life and those jerks will eventually stop bothering me. However, sometimes that doesn't work for me. It makes me feel a little better knowing that some people care about me. I do things I like in order to keep myself busy during the day, but at night and in the mornings, I obsess about

Chapter One

whoever is bugging me to the point that I drive others insane. I hate making others upset, but I also hate the fact that I can't change the people I can't stand. Here's a situation in which I felt that way: I went to a program on the same property as my old high school called CTP or Community Transition Program. It's a class that teaches social and job skills. CTP is the coolest program for mentally disabled, young adults! The teachers are nice, and they explain things in ways we can understand. They also take us on field trips once in a while, and help us on our job sites, as well as teaching us in the classroom. Anyway, the problem I'm about to explain started at this place. Actually, it started a few years ago; but, it came back to haunt me . There was this guy in my class whom I strongly disliked. He was raised in a family where women are secondary to men. I disagree with that since I believe with a passion that men and women are equal (in my family, we treat everyone with respect). Plus, he's an atheist and I'm a Christian. I have a tendency to think that I constantly have to try to persuade people to think the same way as I do. I don't want to act like a dictator; I just want to defend the issues I'm passionate about. I'm learning that I don't always have to be defensive. I'm also learning that no matter how hard I try, I won't get other people to change their ways; unless they want to change themselves. I've learned that others will often react negatively to my persuasions. Nobody likes to be told how to act by someone who's not in charge of them. Anyway, the perpetrator I was just describing didn't just pick on me, he also bothered some other people I know. That bothers me even more! So we really clashed with each other. If only closed minds came with closed mouths! I've gone to school with him since high school. He did lots of little things to get on his classmate's nerves, but I've never forgotten the one thing he said that really got to me. I think I was in either tenth or eleventh grade when going through this episode. It happened in Special Education class during a lecture. Right in the middle of it, this certain male student made a comment that really ticked me off! He said, "Men are better than women at most jobs." I told him firmly, "That is not true. You are being sexist." After that, he and I had a passionate argument about men's and women's rights until the teacher told us to stop. I was close to tackling that boy and making his face bleed! I refrained from doing that, since I'm a good-natured person.

I also didn't attack him because there was a chance that he could be tougher than me. You never know until it happens. I constantly told my parents, teachers, and friends about how much I wanted to get back at him for the awful things he said. I also have trouble with constantly bringing up my past experiences whenever I get mad at someone I don't like. That even happens in the present, when I'm having issues with someone else; which remind me of similar things that happened in the past. It doesn't even have to be someone I don't like. Those bad memories just get triggered some-times. I even had nightmares and stressed about his next moves whenever I had a bad flashback with him in it. Most people just tell those kinds of people how they feel once and then pretend they're not there if they don't listen the first time, but not me. I constantly yell at them and explain my extremely strong emotions to the people I trust. I really do wish that I could have forgotten about him, like average people can. There was this nagging feeling inside of me that told me, *Tia, he will never learn to take women seriously unless you prove him wrong.* This story is proof of what I said before, about how hard I try to get people to agree with me. That boy made me so angry that I had trouble controlling myself. By that I mean raising my voice whenever I talked about him, shaking, stomping, making fists, tightening muscles, hitting stuff, squeezing my stress ball, and sometimes I even had crying meltdowns when alone. Autistic people tend to get a little more upset in situations that make them feel uncomfortable or bad than regular people.

Having sudden outbursts is my way of telling people, "I'm angry, upset, and uncomfortable and I want you to back off!" Most people refer to this type of behavior as throwing tantrums, but I just want to let them know how I'm feeling at the time. I'll explain more about this later. There's stuff I do to distract myself after I calm down, like listening to music, playing computer games, etc. That only works temporarily. When I'm not doing anything, he or whoever else is bugging me comes back to mind. Fortunately, I figured out a way to improve that situation without going psychotic, thinking of ways to torture him, or picking a physical fight. Since I'm into martial arts, and I took Tae Kwon Do in the past; I had a dream one night about using my skills against that boy. I never did that in real life, since I was taught that violence should never be used unless I get attacked. Although, that dream did feel good at the moment!

While I was washing dishes one night, I had a thought. I told my dad, "I just got the best idea!"

"What is it," he asked.

I replied, "You know what I should do about mean people who constantly bother me? I should tell myself, 'Don't pay any attention to them, Tia. People like that thrive off of your reactions. Remember what God, your friends, and your loved ones told you. Karma will eventually catch up with the bad people. You just worry about yourself.' So, I shouldn't stress over it." Dad thought that was a good idea. Sometimes this idea is easier said than done, since I often tend to react without thinking, but I am working on that issue.

Most autistics have a hard time when sudden changes are made in life. Most autistics, me included, tend to feel more comfortable living structured lives in which they get used to routines. Any change in those routines and they would wig out. A good example of that would be, say an autistic person had a dentist appointment, and they had to miss their favorite TV show for it. If they were highly-functioning, they would tell whoever reminded them of the appointment something like, "But, (fill in name of show) starts in (fill in number of minutes or hours)." Over the years, I've learned to become more flexible. I still get disappointed whenever I don't get to do things my way every once in a while, though. Little things like that can

Chapter Two

seem trivial to most people, but to autistics routines are everything. So, the best way to introduce new things to them is to tell them about events; like appointments, ahead of time and walk them through things slowly. That way, it will be easier for them to get used to new plans. The people I know have tried this with me many times and it works. It's definitely easier for me to accept some changes in my routine that way, but sometimes I have to deal with unplanned changes. Like when one of my meetings gets cancelled, because I got sick or something for example. Those times can be difficult, depending on the sudden changes. But sometimes, I'm good at dealing with sudden changes. I never was that way when I was younger. During my childhood, I felt that every single part of my old routine had to be exactly the same.

Also, different people react differently. Behavior really depends on the person. I don't know every autistic person personally. However, I have observed the way I act compared to my classmates throughout most of my life. Some of the people I've met have issues I can relate to. One of them was my best friend. We have known each other since high school. She went to job training with me. Sometimes, we helped each other improve ourselves as well as hanging out. I think that is a good thing. Other people I've seen make me wonder what their issues are until I ask somebody who knows them. I've observed autistic kids who make "weird" noises as a way of communicating. A few kids I used to go to school with did that. There was a boy who rode the same school bus as me who is mostly quiet; except when he repeats stuff he's heard from other people. At first, I thought these types of behaviors were strange; since I have no trouble speaking and I don't say random things out of the blue. But then I learned that these are common behaviors in low-functioning autistic people. I also used to know a girl who was highly-functioning, but she had different challenges than me. This goes to show that even autistic people can be diverse from each other. This is true even when they are put into the same category.

I have a brother, who is six years younger than me. He was born in the year 1994 and I was born in the year 1989. We have always loved each other very much, and always will; even though sometimes we get on each other's nerves. But, it is normal for family members to do that sometimes. I remember when my mom asked me how I felt about getting a sibling. I was very excited and said that I wanted a baby sister, but I got a brother instead; which was ok with me. I ended up loving him anyway. Plus, since not a whole lot of people wanted to be my friends in school at that age; I thought it would be great to have another kid around to play with. When he was a baby, I used to want to hold him and help my mom feed him with a bottle a lot. We used to play with each other as little kids, even though I still kind of kept to myself. I remember one specific photo of us sitting in a cardboard box, in our pajamas; smiling, probably pretending the box was a boat or something. I was six years old and he was one years old in that picture. Sometimes having another kid living in the same house as me, also felt a little strange since before that I was used to being an only child. But eventually, I got used to it.

Now that we're both much older, we don't quite hang out as much as we used to. My brother is now sixteen and I'm twenty-one. We still love each other a lot. It's just that we both like to do our own thing, and our interests are vastly different. For example, he dislikes writing and I like it. He'd rather play video games, which I like to do too; but I don't play the same kinds as him. He plays games like, the "Halo" series and the,

"Fallout" series. I play games more like, "Family Feud"; and I occasionally play ones like, any of the "Tekken" games whenever I get the chance. I also learned that has to do with the fact that our genders are different. It's not that brothers and sisters can never get along or anything. It is just that, siblings of the same gender tend to get closer than those of different genders; because they generally have a lot more in common. There are also some situations where that's not necessarily true, but I don't want to get off topic. Besides differences in interests, etc. our social behaviors and the ways we think are completely opposite too. You see, he doesn't have Autism and I do. He does not have any disabilities, actually. Due to that fact, we often misunderstand each other. This is just one of the many examples of that. Whenever I get frustrated about anything in front of my family members, to them it looks as though I'm angry; even though I haven't quite reached that emotion yet. There are times when I have to be reminded that, there are differences of tones of voice and body language between anger and frustration. Usually when I turn from frustrated into angry I say, "I wasn't angry before, but I am now;" and/or I act even more upset than I was before. I have gotten better at working on my social skills over the years, but sometimes I backtrack. He says that he often feels overwhelmed as my sibling, which I heard happens to a lot of people who have autistic brothers and/or sisters. Sometimes, I get emotionally overwhelmed by things that go on between us as well. He's a nice kid and really mature for his age, but there are times when his typical teenage attitude drives me crazy. Whenever that kind of stuff happens, I often forget that he is still being raised and I get bothered by it. I'm gradually learning how to deal with that, though. Nobody is perfect, but at least my family and I all try our best. And fortunately, we all still spend at least some time together as a family.

A lot of autistic people have some of the same behavioral habits, but every autistic person is still unique. Here is a list of my behavioral habits, and the explanations for them that I did in the past or still do.

1. Rubbing the skin in between my fingers until they're raw: I did this in elementary school very often. The reason for it was, at that time it felt good to me. Until, my parents and teachers noticed that my hands were bleeding; and they asked me to stop. I did stop. I heard that a lot of autistics self-mutilate. They do that because they do repetitive activities in order to self-soothe, not because they are trying to be emo or anything. Trust me, there is a huge difference. I also

Chapter Three

used to do other weird things to myself for various reasons, but I do not want to get into that. It's a good thing I eventually learned to stop doing those things, because I don't want to hurt myself or look like a freak.

2. Bending downward and rubbing my hands; or rubbing my hands in midair: I still do both of those habits. Sometimes, I catch myself and stop. Other times, people who know me have to remind me to quit doing that. I usually do those things when I'm excited, nervous, or while laughing about something really funny.

3. Rocking back and forth: I do this for the same reason as rubbing my hands.

4. Staring off into space: When I do this, it usually means I'm deep in thought. To other people, it may seem as though I am aloof from the world. I am trying not to do that anymore.

5. Rubbing my face: I started doing this recently because it's a nervous habit. A lot of times I'm not aware of doing it until it's brought to my attention. My parents said that, the only reason I should touch my face is when I'm washing it, taking care of acne, blowing my nose, applying make-up or lotion, or scratching

an itch. If I play with it, it could cause acne problems. Plus, it will eventually misshape my appearance. I obviously don't want either of those things to happen to me! I usually make sure to keep my hands busy whenever I can.

6. Echolalia: The definition of this term is repeating stuff you said in a whispering tone right after you said it. I do that frequently. My mom thinks it's creepy when I do that. A lot of times, I don't realize that I'm repeating stuff unless someone tells me, my mother says, "You don't need to whisper the same things you're telling me under your breath." I often do what is called, "thinking out loud" as well as repeating my sentences. My voice also drifts up and down in tone.

7. Constantly telling people what I'm going to do next: A lot of times, I feel like I need to let people know what I'm doing. That way, they could let me know when they need me for something. For instance, Dad might say, "Tia, I need you to go scoop the cat's litter." My answer would be, "Okay, then I'll take a shower and watch a movie." My family members find this one annoying and I'm trying to stop. My parents keep on telling me that I

don't need to tell them every little detail about my life. "Just do it!" Mom often says. But, sometimes I forget.

8. Giving people definitions when they don't need them: This habit pretty much explains itself. The people I know already know that I'm smart. This is one of the ways I like to show it.

9. Giving twenty-minute explanations: When I'm having discussions with people, I sometimes feel like they don't understand me. So, I tend to over-explain the topic of discussion. Most of the time, it takes a while for me to explain myself fully. Most people say, "I get it" after the first few sentences. I used to get upset at them about that a lot. I thought they didn't care about what I had to say. But nowadays, I realize that possibly they have to do or go somewhere important and they don't have time to talk right now, or they really do "get it." Or sometimes, they just don't want to talk about that particular subject for now or not at all. When it's that last reason, I get upset, since I have something I really want to get off my chest. This happens when I'm giving my parents my opinions about something

they already know about me; but they don't want to hear about it unless it's necessary. A good example of that is sex. They accept discussions/questions when needed. But when it comes to stuff like, "I had a dream that I did this with this boy," my folks' replies sound like, "Tell that to your girlfriends! We don't want to know!" Same with other people. Or sometimes, I'll tell others when I feel uncomfortable. But for some odd reason, I forget that when it's the other way around. I have been told that I have a hard time telling when certain conversations and topics are appropriate to discuss with others. For example, family or private matters I have dumped on strangers who don't know that I have Autism.

10. Not ascertaining when I want to talk to someone who's busy: A lot of times, I walk into a room where my parents are, see that they're talking on the phone, doing paperwork, or other things, and I interrupt. I forget to check to see if this is an appropriate time to talk. They get angry, because I don't address them properly and I talk to them from another room; or I start talking in mid-sentence. I have trouble putting myself in other people's

shoes. I assume they know what I'm talking about, when, in fact, they don't. I get frustrated when they react this way, because I feel the need to tell them whatever I have to say at the moment; and I don't like it when people misunderstand me.

11. Arguing over everything and throwing tantrums: A lot of times, I try to discuss things with my family members or others that I know calmly. But, they often turn into heated debates. This is because I try explaining my point of view on certain subjects; but people either disagree with me, or I feel like they don't understand why I feel that way about such-in-such. Or both. Sometimes, my parents ask me why I did certain things whenever I get into trouble. When I try to tell them the answers, they don't really want to know. I don't understand why they do that to me and it makes me really, really frustrated! But then I learned that maybe those are rhetorical questions. I still have a hard time expressing my emotions in ways that aren't considered "argumentative." It's tough to do that when you're angry or disagreeing. I throw tantrums because sometimes I feel like that is the only way to show that

I am angry. I've been doing this for years. I have learned that, it is childish to act that way and I should not be doing that anymore as an adult. Dad gave me a good tip on that. He said that whenever I get angry, I should tell the person that in a firm tone of voice; instead of throwing tantrums. That would be the more mature thing to do in most situations where I get mad. Sometimes it is still hard to remember that when I get caught up in the moment though."

12. Not speaking clearly: Lately, I've been mumbling when I speak. I speak loud and clear the first half of my sentences and then quietly, making it hard for people to barely hear me in the middle of them. I don't realize this unless my family members say, "What? I can't hear you. You're mumbling again." My dad thinks it's because I get nervous when I'm trying to tell people something. I think he's right about that sometimes, but not always. Most of the time, I just do it because it's a habit. I also stammer over my words while changing the volume of my voice from loud to soft. I'm trying to improve on that, since I always want to be heard. If I don't speak up, people aren't going to be able to understand me.

13. Seeming like not wanting to be touched: When I was little, I used to pull away from my family members when they tried to hug me. It's not like I did not want to receive physical affection from them. It is just that I wanted space at the same time as wanting human contact. A lot of autistics have this issue since they mostly like to keep to themselves, including me. It takes time to break away from that type of behavior. Also, this doesn't just have to do with receiving hugs or kisses from family members. It also has to do with other kinds of touching, like hand shakes, pats on the back, etc. Over the years, I came to accept and sometimes even welcome certain kinds of physical contact from others. There are times when I even offer to hug my family members, or to give shorter hugs to good friends when needed. It is a good thing I've changed in that way, because I do not want to seem emotionally distant. Especially, when I am going to be in an intimate and romantic relationship with a man someday.

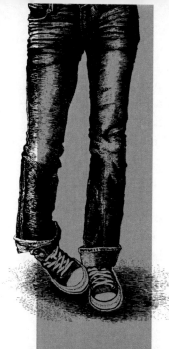

E ven in my later years, I still struggle with some of my old issues, but I think I have come a long way since I was younger. I still am very obsessive. An example of that would be the story about the boy who bothered me. I still remembered him, long after he moved to another state, because I still had to go to class with his friend. He is just like him in many ways. I got help with getting over that. I forgot to mention that my obsessive behavior also applies to things I'm interested in, as well as things that upset me. For example, let's just say one of my parents said they might do something fun with me like shopping. After that, I nag everybody about it because I feel excited about something nobody's sure about. I also have a hard time letting things

Chapter Four

go whenever I'm promised something and it doesn't happen. It's very hard for a lot of autistics, me included, to let things go; as I have described a few times throughout this book. I'm slowly learning not to worry about the small stuff. There are also many other things I have improved on over the years.

For years, I have struggled with managing my time effectively. When I was in school, I missed a lot of buses since I never liked to be rushed in the mornings. I often thought that I had a lot of time to get ready, even when I had to hurry up. Every once in a while, I still go through similar situations, even though I have since learned how to tell time; with both a digital and an analog clock. A long time ago, I used to only be able to tell time if someone else set my digital clock and watch for me. I also could not figure out things like, how long it takes to get to a place; or what time I was supposed to be there. Sometimes, I still have trouble figuring out those types of things. But, at least I'm learning. My family members have told me at least a thousand times, "The world does not revolve around Tia Marie." It took me a while to learn that, in order to get by in life; I sometimes have to go by other people's schedules, as well as my own. A lot of times, it seems as though autistic people live in a world of their own; and other people are just buzzing around them. It takes time to teach them that, the world does not work that way.

I also still have a little trouble paying attention. One time when I was baking chocolate chip cookies, I let my mind drift off to another place; while I was waiting for them to cook. I was so oblivious that day. I ended up burning those cookies so badly, that they stuck together and turned black. Since then, I have learned to pay attention to what I am doing at the moment; no matter what is on my mind. There are times when I still slip up in that area. Everybody has those kinds of days. But compared to how I was at paying attention as a little girl, I would say I have become a lot more aware of the world around me.

I grew up in the nineties when people were just discovering Autism. Well actually, I think they found it somewhere in the late eighties or some earlier decade. I watched the movie "Rain Man," which is the oldest piece of evidence about Autism that I know of. That movie was made in the year 1988. It's not only a good film, but it also taught me a little bit more about Autism through one of the main characters. The character I'm speaking of is a highly functioning autistic man named Raymond. Maybe you readers should rent this movie.

These are some of the stories my parents told me about myself. When I was a small child, I acted bizarrely. I stood in front of moving swings and slides on playgrounds. I don't know why I did that. My father told me that while common sense came naturally to other children, I had to learn it. I wasn't very good at paying attention to my surroundings for years, but now I'm much better at that. Here's a story about something my parents had to go through while raising me. In elementary school, my teachers constantly called my parents and asked if they could talk about my behavior and/or asked them to pick me up. The teachers didn't know what to do with me since I acted so weird and often got out of control. One of the things I did was I sat under desks and hooted like an owl. That doesn't sound familiar to me, since I stopped acting that way a long time ago. One time, my mom and dad went to a parent-teacher conference. I was in second grade at the time. I wasn't at the meeting, but my parents just recently informed me that a school psychologist stated to them, "Your daughter needs to get her act together or else she won't be allowed in this school." When they heard that, my parents were furious! They had to explain my disability and fight for me for several years! Especially since back then I wasn't able to tell people myself. Now, I still have a little bit of trouble communicating sometimes, but at least I can advocate for myself a lot more than in the past. After my parents told me that story, I thought, "That was harsh and ignorant! I can't believe she said that!" This totally uncalled for statement inspired the title of my memoir. Actually, my dad came up with the title, but that's why I decided to use his idea.

Thank God in the twenty-first century people figured out a lot more about Autism and how to deal with autistic people! The only downsides are, there's still no knowledge about the origin or cure; it's often mistaken for other mental disabilities, it's not something anybody can grow out of, and it's now an epidemic. Statistics have shown that when people discovered Autism, it used to be found in very few. Nowadays, many people, adults included, are being diagnosed with Autism. Another interesting fact about this disability is that it's more prominent in boys than girls. I was one of the rare cases. Now, more girls are showing signs of Autism. The statistics used to show that, one in every ten thousand kids were diagnosed with Autism and four out of five were boys. Now, it's one in every one hundred and ten kids and this epidemic is still spreading.

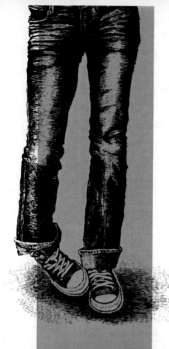

For many years, Autism has affected me educationally as well as socially. I fell behind in some subjects, while excelling in others. It took me several years to learn math and telling time. It took me until last year to get the concept of counting change back. When I was in high school, I had to take Basic Math since I had so much trouble with that in the grades average people learn it in. I'm proud to say that I have improved dramatically in both subjects over the years. I still need a calculator to solve some problems, but that's mostly because I volunteered at Allenmore Hospital gift shop. That job required me to move a little quickly while dealing with customers. It also helped me understand how to give back the correct amount of change. Before that, I got really

Chapter Five

frustrated at my family members when they asked me math, time, and money questions. I could figure out even numbers in all three subjects but, when it came to odd numbers, I got super confused. Now that people have explained those subjects in ways I can understand, I can solve problems with a lot more ease than back then. I still get stuck once in a while though, and that's okay, since everybody has different strengths and weaknesses. While I was in high school, I loved World History class, since I like studying about different cultures. I had almost no trouble with learning the materials in that class. However, I had to work a little bit at U.S. History, since I thought World History was way more interesting. I'm not being anti-patriotic by saying that, it's just hard for most people to memorize materials from subjects that they deem "dull."

Can you believe that I used to hate writing until fifth grade? I couldn't either, since I always loved reading and always had been very good at it. Plus, I've been good at spelling and pronunciation for a long time. When I was in elementary school, I read above grade level and reading only improved over the years. My parents used to read to me a lot when I was little and it made me happy. That's how I came to love books. At age three, I taught myself how to read by reading signs during car rides. My mom and dad helped me a little bit too. But for some odd reason, I refused to write sentences when my teachers told me to. They used to have to bribe me with reading time in order to teach me how to write. I thought that reading was way more fun than writing. It was only during middle school in fifth grade when I changed my mind. In Special Education class, after reading a fictional story I really enjoyed, there was an assignment at the end of it that told me to write a story about a magic carpet. Even though I disliked writing, I loved being creative. That was evident when I did art projects and drew pictures in school and at home. I decided to do that assignment. When I finished my first book, I was so thrilled that I thought, *I didn't know that books came from people writing them until now! I want to become a writer when I grow up!* I should've thought that statement through before telling my thought to others. Sometimes, I still say things that don't make sense. What I meant to say was, "I didn't know writing could be a good hobby and career for me until now." A lot of people with mental disabilities have problems with speaking before thinking. Even average people make that mistake sometimes. I'm working on that, though. Before I wanted to become an author, I wanted to be a cartoonist, since I liked drawing a lot more back then than I do now. Ever since that moment, I've been studying about becoming an author and I also discovered that fiction writing was my passion. I've always been more entertained by creative stories than true ones. However, this book about my life as an autistic person is of interest to many people who are curious about this mental disorder. Popularity in books, as in anything, changes with time. It's very difficult to get any type of story published, whether it's fiction or nonfiction, but I'm still determined to succeed. Another thing that I learned about becoming an author is you have to pass English class. Otherwise, publishing companies won't accept your manuscripts. I got decent grades in that course, but there were still some subjects within that class that I had trouble understanding. One of those things was pieces of literature that were written in Old English. I had to get a lot of extra help from my teachers to translate those works.

When I was in 9th grade, I took an Independent Living class. Not only did the teacher teach the class some skills they need in order to live on their own, like cooking and cleaning skills. She also taught the class how to take care of babies, in case of unplanned pregnancies; or just if the kids wanted to raise families someday. She taught this life lesson by, assigning everyone computerized baby dolls; which do almost everything that a real infant does. The only things they didn't do were, using their diapers; spitting up, moving, hearing things, and feeling different temperatures. The only way you could tell if they went potty is, attaching a "clean" diapers magnet to a hole in the back; after frantically trying everything else to make it stop crying. Then, if you figured out what it needed help with it would make a cooing sound. It would also do that while it was sleeping every once in a while, to let you know that it is content. The babies also made different sounding cries for each need, which was tough to figure out at first. The only one I learned right away was the extremely loud one which means, "You're hurting me;" by either shaking it or letting the head fall too far back, etc. One thing which was really odd about the project was, the students got to choose their baby's gender and race. This does not happen in real life. My guess is the teacher probably said that to make the students a little more comfortable with this assignment, which was not the point of it. But, at least I learned some things about babies. Boy, were those things a challenge. I think mine must have been sick or something, because I had to feed it and change the doll's diapers a lot more than normal. The baby kept waking everybody in my family up in the middle of the night, which real babies do too. I also messed up a few times, and had to ask for help from my mother every once in a while. But overall, I would say I was a good mother to it. I got a "B+" on the project. There were also cute parts about the doll, as well as annoying parts about it. I remember that mine was a baby girl. She was kind of adorable looking, for a doll with a computer chip in its back. I chose an Asian baby and gave her a cute sounding Chinese name, Mei-Mei. During those four days the project lasted for, I treated Mei- Mei like she was my own daughter. I even dressed her in my old baby doll clothes (which surprisingly fitted) and rocked her softly whenever she cried hysterically. I also never let her leave my sight, except for the time when I accidentally left her on the school bus the first day. Fortunately though, I called the bus company and got her back. Before this project, I wasn't sure of whether I wanted to become a mother as an adult or not. But after it was over, I decided to never have children. And this is not just because I don't want to go through labor, or deal with hectic adoption legalities. I love kids and all, but they're way too much of a handful for me. And as they get older, there are still tough issues to face even though they get a little easier to take care of. Like for example, what if your kid decides to start believing in something you're strongly against? Or a more common example would be; how would you answer those awkward questions when your kids reach puberty? Those kinds of things are difficult even for an average parent to handle. So, just imagine how hard that would be for a person with Autism.

Now that I explained how Autism affected me educationally, here are some things that affected me socially. When I was younger, I took everything literally. My speech therapists had to teach me idioms for a long time. As I got older, I learned when people are using figures of speech or just kidding with me. Sometimes, I still take things literally when I'm unaware of jokes or figures of speech. At least I'm a little more aware of those things now than I was when I was younger. I also have trouble with separating fantasy from reality. When I was a little girl, I used to believe that movies and TV were real. It took me a longer time than most kids to learn about camera tricks and stunt people. I also got overly worked up about characters that I didn't like.

I remember when I watched a cartoon in which a raccoon was a thief. In real life, that animal does show that kind of behavior, but not in the same way as a human. Whenever I watched that cartoon, I saw that particular character in black-and-white clothing and a mask stealing stuff from the good guys and thought that was really how raccoons acted. After a while, I learned that that was a silly thing to think. I also learned that the only thing that's real on TV is the news, most of the time, and educational channels. Once in a while, I will see an entertaining show that is real, like "Extreme Home Makeover" for example. But, most TV shows are fake. Same with films. Some of them are based on true stories, while most of them are just screenplays; which are either original or based on someone's short story or novel. Sometimes, I still feel for the characters in the movies and TV shows I watch or the books I read. But, that's not because I think those stories are true. I just happen to be a very passionate person who's also a good writer. Artistic people tend to feel their emotions a little more intensely than others, no matter what kind of art they create. Also, being an autistic person contributes to that personality trait. Or, at least it does for me and some other autistic people.

When I was in junior high through high school, I participated in extra curricular activities which included special needs people. At the U.P. Public Library, there was an anime club I used to go to during my high school years. It was not specifically for special needs people, but they let me in anyway. I enjoyed that a lot since there were people there who shared a common interest with me, and most of them were nice. Too bad I only was allowed to go there until I turned 18. I also used to be on a Special Olympics team called, U.P. Pride. We did track, basketball and bowling. My favorite sport was, bowling. I am usually not much of a sports fan but, I had fun while I was on that team; since I made friends while I was doing those activities. Before I heard about Special Olympics, I had trouble fitting in at school because of my disability; even though I never had any problems with having a diverse group of friends. That does not really matter, as long as we have things in common and that those friends are good ones. Being a part of U.P. Pride made me feel like I belonged somewhere outside of my family. I got the same kind of feeling when I joined a youth group, at Olympic View Baptist Church near my old house; in University Place. Anyway, at the youth group everybody (not just disabled kids) between the ages of 13 and 18 were allowed in the club. We not only learned about God, but we also played games like dodge ball, and video games; had snacks and parties, and went on fun trips. One of the best times I spent with my youth group was, the first time I went inter-tubing in the snow in Snoqualmie. When I got to 12th grade, I was a little sad to learn that I had to quit those clubs I used to participate in. At least I still have those good memories, though. Also, I've joined groups for adults since then. Like Safe Relationships classes, and the S.T.A.R.S. program for example. My Safe Relationships class is good for me since there is still a lot to learn about that. I also like the S.T.A.R.S. program since it helps me learn how to advocate for myself. We also get to do fun things sometimes, like last year's X-Mas party. Plus, those things get me out of the house. I wish there was more interesting groups, like an anime club; or something else I'm interested in for adults with disabilities. Unfortunately, there aren't very many groups like that; but hopefully there will be more in the future. I'm also open to joining social clubs and classes with average people, as long as I feel welcome at those places.

I mostly kept to myself and was very shy when I was younger. I wasn't very good at standing up for myself whenever people bothered me. I would just keep it all bottled up inside until I exploded in small ways. I used to know a very mean girl who always picked on me at recess in elementary school. The story about her began like this...

I used to love playing the game tetherball whenever I got a chance at school. I got a natural high from hitting the ball around the pole. That's because I liked spinning things. I even used to get on the ball and swing around the pole like it was a carnival ride. After a while, I learned that was dangerous. I was so good at tetherball that I beat almost everybody who challenged me. Then, one day, a girl, who I think was

Chapter Six

in a higher grade than me, came up to the tetherball court and beat me for the first time. To me, she looked really intimidating, since she was twice my size and she never smiled. She was as scary as she looked too. Even though I was nothing but nice to her, she never acted friendly toward me. Whenever we played tetherball against each other, she was too aggressive with the ball. Even off the tetherball court, she would tease and taunt me. That's probably because I was a weaker person back then than I am now, but that doesn't mean I deserved to be treated like dirt. I was too afraid of this bully to show her how I felt. Instead, I constantly stressed and obsessed about the things she did to me. I also worried about the things she was going to do to me next. My parents and teachers were really concerned about me whenever I told them about this problem child. My parents tried teaching me how to deal with bullies, but there was no avoiding or stopping that girl! My hidden emotions showed in the angry drawings my teachers and folks found. The drawings were of her head as a tetherball and me smacking it around. I was so obsessed that I even practiced tetherball when nobody was around; so that I could beat her the next time we played. While playing, I imagined her head was the ball and I punched it so hard that it flew high over the pole and created wounds on my hands. I did this for several minutes a day each day. Then, something horrible happened! After all that unhealthy practice, I finally beat her at tetherball; but she was a sore loser. When I shouted excitedly several times, "I won!" the bully pulled me over to the tire structure, held me up against it, and choked me! I wasn't able to defend myself, since she was stronger than me. So I just struggled, screamed, and cried until a playground monitor stopped her! I wish I was mature enough to handle martial arts back then, because I could've used it at that moment.

I tried to get back at her one time by giving her some Atomic Fireball candies. They were these super spicy, cinnamon flavored, hard balls that you had to suck on. I thought they would burn the roof of her mouth off. They sure did mine! However, my sneaky little scheme didn't work. She actually liked hot foods! *Dang it, I was hoping to get her,* I thought. Oh well, at least now I laugh about that incident, and at least I learned to be a little more assertive. The next story involves martial arts … and I don't mean I took a few classes then went back to beat up the bully!

When I was very young, I wanted to take Ballet since I liked to dance and listen to music. I thought it would be a fun thing to learn. I also always enjoyed girly things. I still do, mostly. After a couple of classes, however, I quit my lessons when I found out the dance was extremely tough to master. Not too long after that, I discovered something I found way more intriguing than Ballet. It was Karate. One of my parents introduced me to a really fun Super Nintendo game entitled, "Street Fighters II." It's one of those games where you choose from several different characters, travel to levels that look like foreign countries, and kick other character's butts. That game was so addicting! Unfortunately, I wasn't able to keep it for very long. I watched the characters in my favorite video game and decided that I wanted to be just like them … which turned out to be a very bad thing. At that age, I didn't know that violence is not okay. Eventually, my parents had to take my game away. They were afraid I was going to imitate the characters and hurt somebody. By the way, this happened during elementary school. For a while, I felt upset since I really enjoyed "Street Fighters II." (Interesting fact: That's also how I got good at video games. I also played non-violent games like "Super Mario Bros.," etc.).

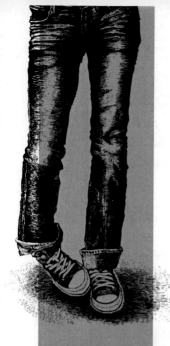

Not too long after the "Street Fighters II" episode, one of my teachers in special education class found out that I'm into martial arts and gave me a book entitled *Three Ninjas Kick Back*. It was a story based on an old movie about three boys who looked about the same age as me at the time who learned Karate from their grandfather. That became my favorite book. Like the game I mentioned in the last chapter, I lost my privileges to that book too. That was kind of sad, but at least I eventually learned my lesson. After I realized how badly I was behaving, my folks gave me my stuff back. When I made it to intermediate school, I asked Mom and Dad if I could take some form of martial arts. My parents told me they didn't want me to take martial arts classes until I

Chapter Seven

became older. They thought I was still too immature to handle any kind of self-defense courses. They were right. Whenever I went to the school's library, I secretly borrowed any kind of martial arts books I could get my hands on. You know that old saying about how parents have eyes in the back of their heads? Well, it's true. As soon as they found out I was sneaking around, they informed all my teachers not to let me read any more of those books. However, I've always been a clever girl, so I hid where the teachers and librarian couldn't see me and secretly read martial arts-related books. I'm not proud of being defiant, but I'm glad that I developed that interest, since I was able to pursue it way later in life. A few years ago, my parents let one of their friends, a martial arts teacher, teach me a few things during the summer. He was a great master. He not only taught me how to protect myself, but I also learned self-discipline and how to be aware of my surroundings. The martial art that I mostly studied was Tae Kwon Do. My parent's friend taught me what is called Melee Combat; which is a combination of Tae Kwon Do, Karate, Kung Fu, Wrestling and Boxing. I became really good at it and received a green belt. Unfortunately, my master had to retire due to a back surgery. He's been participating in competitions for practically his whole life, so that must've taken a toll on his body in the long run. I had to give up martial arts because my parents and I couldn't find another decent instructor. Hopefully, someday I will be able to go back to doing martial arts. That would be a good thing to learn since I want to travel the world if I become well-known enough of an author to afford it. The next type of martial arts I want to learn is Kung Fu, since that's the most impressive one I see in most of the martial arts movies I watch. My favorite is, "Crouching Tiger, Hidden Dragon." Plus, it's featured in the fighting video games I play once in a while. It's also the one that started all other types of martial arts. You'll have to find another source to learn the history, because it's way too long for me to write down. Getting into martial arts is what got me into Asian cultures. After seeing the movie, "The Last Emperor," I became fascinated with other aspects of Asian cultures. It's interesting how people sometimes find new interests within current ones, if they're connected that is. I got tired of that movie after a while, but I still love other Asian movies and many other things that are related to those cultures; like Japanese animation for example. They call it anime, by the way.

On a completely different subject, I used to have an abnormal fear of going to the doctor's office. Just the year before last year, I freaked out so bad before going in for my annual physical that I threw up! This is what I used to do every time I got extremely nervous. I also had crying tantrums, bad dreams, and had trouble focusing on positive things at school and home. I've had this phobia since I was a little girl because I hated getting shots, getting my blood tested, and the suspense that came with waiting to get those two things done. When I was a child, I used to hide from the nurse behind the door of the room whenever I had to get a shot. I also worried about whether I was going to come out healthy or sick. I always came out fine and always used to tell my parents, "That wasn't so bad." Actually, it took me several years to learn that it really isn't as terrifying as I made it out to be. I even faked my period in order to get out of a female exam once. I got in really big trouble for that trick! Whenever I need to see a doctor now, I still experience anxiety attacks, but they're only minor compared to the fits I've had in the past. Volunteering in a hospital after senior year helped lessen my fear as well as maturing and remembering the things people I know told me about it. What also helps me calm down is a list of tips to help me relax in any stressful situation; not just visiting the doctor. Here it is below:

Tia's Relaxation Tips

1. Listen to soft music on my Mp3 player (It makes me think of beautiful scenery).

2. Think of things I like (i.e. cats).

3. Think of a reward for good behavior when (blank) is over (i.e. watching my favorite movie when I get home).

4. Bring my purse or my squishy ball to take the bad energy out of me (Whenever I squeeze something during a painful or stressful event, it takes some of the mental and physical pressure away).

5. Repeat either phrase:

   "It's okay, Tia. You'll still be alive when (blank) is over."

   "Be tough, like a martial arts warrior."

6. Think of what my parents/grandma would say or do in my situation.

7. Don't worry, be happy. Think of the positive side of things (Everything has a positive side). Example: I went to the doctor, which I don't care for, but he found a broken bone and fixed it and now I feel better.

Dad suggested the last two tips. My parents have the best advice. They always know exactly what to say in every situation I come to them for. I like the phrase, "Don't worry, be happy" from tip number seven; even though the song can get a little annoying after a while. Wouldn't it be nice if the world was stress-free and pleasant all the time? Number six is also one of my favorite tips on that list, because of my parent's good advice; but also because when my grandmother was still alive, she was always there for me. She passed away in the year 2001 and I still miss her and love her a lot, but at least she's in a better place. I'll be able to visit her when I get to Heaven, but in the meantime I'll be here on earth, living every minute of my life and enjoying at least most of it. Grandma would definitely not want me to waste my time on things/people that disturb me; and I know I'd rather spend it on loved ones/friends and things I take pleasure in. So, I'm going to remind myself of that, plus other advice I've received over the years whenever I feel the need for self-improvement.

I often tend to take little things as personal attacks. For example, when I was in high school, one of my math teachers let me play my favorite type of music for the class while we worked. I played one of my favorite Chinese artists, Twelve Girls Band. Since world music isn't the most popular genre, the other students made fun of it, which hurt my feelings. They also called me "weird" because I listened to some types of music they weren't used to. But, I shouldn't have held that grudge as long as I did. Whenever I remember that memory now, I sometimes get upset as if it just happened not too long ago; but I'm learning to shrug it off. This is part of my obsessive behavior I wrote about earlier in this book. Kids can be cruel. However, even though those kids were being rude about the way they expressed their thoughts; they are still entitled to their own opinions. Even today, I still have problems with accepting that every once in a while, even if it's not about other people picking on me. I'm also still learning that people aren't always going to side with me, and that doesn't mean that nobody will ever agree with me. Sometimes I still feel alone when I'm the only one saying anything. We all do. I heard from somewhere that these problems are part of my disability, which can be improved. I also misunderstand some things people say to me and take offense to them. This often happens when I don't pay attention, but I'm learning from my mistakes.

I like a variety of music, unlike most people, who only like one kind. I also have my own musical preferences, like everyone else does; but I still give new genres and artists a chance before I decide whether I like or dislike them. On the plus side, I know a few people who accept things that are a little exotic.

This is something some of my early teachers came up with to control my "odd" behavior. My teachers couldn't handle me, but my parents wanted me to stay in that school. I'm talking about the one where the school psychologist said I would have been expelled from if I didn't shape up. I got kicked out of the other ones I went to before that particular elementary school. The teachers at those other buildings couldn't figure me out either. So, the teachers I had in second through fourth grade tried to figure out some way to control me whenever I went crazy. There was a box-like room built for me. It was named "The Blue Room" because of the dark blue color of the safety padding on the walls, floor, and the back of the door. This just describes the inside of this gigantic box. The

Chapter Eight

outside of it was purely wood and metal. Anyway, the teachers would lock me up inside "The Blue Room" whenever I had hysterical fits. They didn't do this to torture me, like I felt like they did. The teachers just needed to separate me from the other students and staff members until I calmed down. But back then, I didn't think of it that way. I hated "The Blue Room," and took it as a punishment when it actually wasn't. It was pretty effective most of the time. I thought that my teachers were confining me to a cage for the rest of the day. I tried every possible way I could think of to escape. I kicked, punched, rammed, and pushed against the walls to try to knock them down, but the structure was too strongly built. I also screamed my head off, since I thought fussing would make my teachers free me. I even tried to climb out of there unsuccessfully. Finally, when my parents came to pick me up, I gave up and sat in the middle of the floor, calmly waiting for someone to let me out. As I grew up, whenever I remembered this story, I felt glad that my old teachers found a way to soothe me or else I would've ended up living in a mental institution. I still feel that way.

I was digging around in a bin where I kept all my old stories and I found one you might find interesting. Here are some excerpts from a book

I wrote when I was thirteen entitled, *The Story of My Life*.

> "Let's start way back when I was in preschool. I had a whole lot of fun there. I still lived in the old house that was right next to my dad's auto wrecking shop at that time. I thought that it was the greatest place to live because I had lots of fun there as well as school. Except for the only part that I didn't like about it was when I went to bed at nighttime. That part was a little bit scary to me. I used to believe that there were these little black-and-white creatures called, "Moonlights" that liked to lurk around in my room and scare me when they make sudden movements every night. I also used to believe that they lived on the moon during the day, but then they would come down to the earth at night so that they could have fun freaking me out. But now that I'm much older, I know that there isn't anything to be afraid of because moonlights are not real except for if they are the different kind than what I was talking about."

I'm sorry about any grammar or wording errors. I'm clearly better at writing now than I was back then, but I do not want to correct them since they're a piece of history; so bear with me.

Besides, at least they're still readable. It's typical for little kids to be afraid of the dark for one ridiculous reason or another. I don't think anyone else has ever been afraid of what I just described. I also learned that moonlight is just light coming from the sun, when it goes behind the moon at night; and it reflects off of some things. Also, when I am really tired sometimes my eyes trick me into thinking objects are moving at night when they are actually not. Here's another excerpt.

> "My worst fear is roller coasters. It always has been and always will be. Except for if I decide that one of them looks fun to me. Then, that's when I would ride them once in a while. One of my favorite things to do when I was little was either play with my toys in my room, watch a movie, or go outside and play with my dog, Tosha. (Later in life, I figured out that her name was spelled like Tasha). I used to play with her every time I came home from school on the bus from kindergarten to first grade. She was my most favorite dog in the whole wide world. But one day, unfortunately, she perished after getting into the cabinets in the kitchen under the sink; and she started to drink anti-freeze for cars, and it poisoned her. So, that's how she died. Everybody was really sad after that happened."

I remember that as being my first experience with death when I found out what happened to my pet. I still get a little sad whenever I think about it, but I always cheer myself up afterward. Although roller coasters aren't one of my worst fears anymore, I'm still afraid of some of them, like the ones that have loops for example. They make me sick just watching them. In the next chapter, there will be more excerpts.

I've mentioned some pets I've had in the past (Tasha, Petunia, and I forgot to list the others; but that's ok). However, I didn't mention what it feels like to own the pets I have currently. I have a cat named Baby Kiwi, a dog named Halo, and some fish with no names. It's a big responsibility for my family members and I to take care of and love them all, but it's also a good way for my brother and I to learn how to handle the pets we might buy in the future. Currently, all we do is feed them, clean up after them and give them attention. But pretty soon, we're going to have to do a lot more than that for them. It's also fun to have pets sometimes. Most domesticated animals love and play with their owners, especially dogs and cats. The other cool things about having those kinds of pets are, most dogs will try to protect you if you're being attacked by another person or animal in front of them. Also, both dogs and cats can sense some human emotions and they love you unconditionally most of the time. Sometimes when I feel sick or sad, my dog or cat will keep me company and cheer me up. This doesn't always happen but, when it does it makes me feel a little better. Even though I'm more of a cat person, and that's the type of pet I want when I move out; I still love pretty much all of the pets I had and still have in my life. But before I take responsibility for another life, I will have to get the hang of living on my own.

This one is about a pet I got shortly after Tasha passed away.

"I remember when I used to have a pot bellied pig for a pet named Petunia. She was a comical little thing. The funniest moment that I remember was when it was time for her to take a bath; because she would always jump right out of the tub and go running around. I laughed like crazy when that happened!"

"I could also remember the times when I seemed to be a little troublemaker too. One of those times was the first time that I stole something in pre-school and I didn't know better so I got away with it. The time that I stole it was at snack time in school. It was a sugar

Chapter Nine

cookie with pink frosting, and I stole half of (name withheld's) cookie because I wanted to have more after I was done and I didn't know that stealing was wrong at that age, so I didn't get into trouble. There was also the time when I went over to where my cousin used to live and I went and played with her for a little while. But I didn't like it though. I didn't like it because (name withheld) used to be selfish and self-centered when she was little. So, I didn't get to do anything over there without her fussing at me and I was always glad to get away from her when my dad came to pick me up. So, you know what I did to get back at her even though I didn't know what getting back was until later in life? The next time that I came with my dad to visit, I brought my Ken doll with me when my cousin wasn't there at the apartment and I put her Barbie pants on my doll; and stole them from her when it was time to leave after I played dolls for a little while. Boy was she upset when she found out that that happened! I was happy about it though, because I actually thought that she got what she deserved for treating me mean like that. But nowadays, I don't steal from her anymore, because we've become best buddies now that we're a lot older than we were when we were little kids."

Fortunately, that particular cousin isn't a brat anymore. Then again, I haven't seen her in years, so changes could have been made that I don't know about. The reason I didn't tell my parents about how she used to pester me until I got caught with the Barbie pants was because of my passive-aggressiveness. That was also the time when I learned that stealing is wrong. Here's an excerpt about some horrible camping experiences and the things I did to spice them up. These events probably happened when I was either in third or fourth grade.

"My nana had always loved to take me on camping trips. Sometimes I liked them, but other times I didn't. I think that the time when we went to Mt. Leavenworth was the worst. I mean it was a beautiful view and I liked the resort, but the only thing was it took so dang long for us to go back home that my older cousin, (name withheld), and I wanted to go home so bad that we decided to run away and take the van with us. But we only talked about it and planned, so we didn't do it. There was also this one time when I went camping again with my nana and my cousin, and I did one of the biggest, most dangerous and most adventurous thing ever! One day, when I asked my nana if I could take her little Yorkie dog named

Cricket for a walk, I went off to the lodge that was really far away from the campsite, when I was only supposed to go around the block and come back. And do you know what I did when I got there? Well, first I explored all the shops and the restaurant at the lodge, then I climbed all the way to the top floor and out onto the roof! And I had Cricket by her leash the whole way! Boy, was I busted for that! My nana was so worried about me that she had to call the park ranger to drive me back to the campsite. After that, I got into trouble with my nana and my parents for wandering off like that and climbing onto a roof where somebody at the lodge had to get Cricket and I down. I was glad that my life was saved when I was little, because if I would've fallen from the roof, I would've busted my neck or died. It's a good thing that I was careful enough to prevent myself from doing that."

I think I did that because of the fact that I used to believe that movies are real, and in some of the movies, I watched the heroes would do death-defying stunts that real people can't do without getting injured or killed. I was also really bored on that trip, since there weren't very many kid-friendly activities where we stayed, so I decided to do the craziest thing off the top of my head. This, by the way, was also one of the dumbest mistakes I've ever made. At least I learned from (and survived) it. It's also a good thing that my older cousin and I didn't go through with our sneaky plan. I also was relieved that nothing happened to Cricket on the roof.

H ere's one more excerpt from my book, *The Story of My Life:*

"The last thing that I want to tell you about was my first fist fight at Camp Laugh in a Half. I did this when I was eleven years old. It was a fine day at camp, and I was at recess outside at an elementary school (By the way, I edited these excerpts a little bit to prevent personal information from getting out and to remove fluff that I don't need for this book). I was sitting on the big toy talking to a counselor about a dream that I had the night before. That is, until (name withheld) just had to butt into the conversation and call me a name that, well you really don't want to know. Anyway, she thought that I said something that I

Chapter Ten

really didn't say. So I got up, put my fists up at her and said, "You take that back you wretch!" Then I started hitting, kicking, pushing, and slapping her, you know beating her up. Then, she started pushing and kicking me. So after that, I did it right back to her. I was so angry and insulted that I could've beaten her to a bloody pulp. But I didn't. I didn't even bother to hit her face because after all, it was my first fist fight so; I wasn't a professional at it. But, I still won the fight because I did many quick, strong, and hard moves on her body."

I got kicked out of camp for that, even though she was the one who kept on bothering everybody, and that's what made me blow up at her. I regret what I did to her, though. Later in life, I learned that I could have handled that problem in a non-violent way.

These are a couple stories about what it was like for me to become a teenager. When I was in sixth grade, my special education teacher taught the class a little bit about sexual education. She separated the boys and girls to watch videos about what happens when kids hit puberty. The teacher didn't give us much of a "sex talk," because most teachers felt that it wasn't their responsibility to discuss that kind of stuff with their students. To this day, most of them still think that should be the parent's responsibility; which is true to some extent. Some parents are irresponsible, and kids need to be informed before they get themselves into trouble; and if they already did, they need all the help they can get. Anyway, I started going through some of the changes before that lesson and my parents taught me about them. They continued to teach me all they felt I needed to know at that age after the lesson as well. I was really immature back then compared to now. My parents requested that the teachers only teach me about the female side of the discussion, so that I wouldn't be confused about why my body and emotions were dramatically changing. As for the male side of the discussion, I had to wait until I was a little older and more mature to learn about that. That didn't stop me from being curious though. An example of how I used to be immature about that subject would be after the middle school sex education class, I asked my teacher if I could watch the boy's side of the tape. She said "no" to me, because of what my parents told her to do with me during that difficult time. In response, I threw a tantrum like a three-year-old; and screamed, "But, I'm curious!" This type of behavior is abnormal for teens. That is a perfect example of my Autism.

In sixth grade, I was really mystified about boys. There were some male celebrities I used to think were attractive, like the guys from the boy band, N'SYNC for example. I also used to like their music as well as their looks, but I am not a fan of them anymore. They really changed the way I saw boys, but I cannot remember if I was infatuated with any guys in middle school before 7th grade.

In seventh grade, I had my first crush. This was the year when I really started getting boy crazy and discarded most of the interests I had as a little girl. I went through all the normal symptoms of infatuation, except when I threw-up every morning for months, anticipating about seeing this boy in class all night before that. I had a real problem with anxiety back then and sometimes I still do. It took me a long time to learn that throwing up for no good reason is bad for my health. My parents told me that what I was feeling was lovesickness, even though it was just puppy love. I wish I would've gotten that through my head sooner than I did, but at least I didn't suffer from throat or organ damage due to the barfing.

Seventh grade was also the year when I got my heart broken by a boy for the first time. The guy was in my Language Arts class and he didn't feel the same way about me. But even though he told me that, I still liked him. I pursued him for most of the school year. I did every old trick in the book to get him to like me back, including talking constantly to other people about him, admiring him from afar, and writing a love letter addressed to him; which I handed to another girl to give to him at lunch. I even tried sharing some candy I got as a reward from a teacher with him. Even though I didn't mean to, I annoyed him every single school day. Until one day, he decided he had enough of me. When I tried giving him half of my Jolly Ranchers in class, he kept on passing them back to my desk and it turned into a few-minute-passing-cycle. After that, he finally exclaimed angrily, "I don't like you!" I felt so hurt by his reaction that I started crying hysterically, right in front of everybody in the classroom. That was humiliating, but at least I learned not to keep pursuing someone who isn't interested in me. I also learned other things about relationships, etc. as I got older, but that's not what this book is about. I have always had problems deciphering social cues. Like when I had my first crush, for example. When the boy started sending signals that he did not like me back, I didn't get that until he said it verbally. That is just one of the many examples. There have been other times when I missed social cues. A lot of autistics have similar problems. Also, even though I got rejected more times than that; the first time still feels like one of the toughest whenever I remember it. I'm not as sad about those moments as I used to be though, if you know what I mean. Plus, I still have faith that God will one day bring me my "Mr. Right." But in the meantime, I'll keep trying to control myself both physically and emotionally whenever I think of attractive men. I heard that great relationships have both love and sex in them and I believe that is true. Those things have been my biggest obsessions for years, and I still kind of have that problem every once in a while. Fortunately, I've found ways to control myself in that way; but those stories are too personal. I only wrote what was necessary about that difficult transition in my life. Also, even though I learned about and reached puberty, I still wondered why I started getting into boys, since I used to think most of them were mean and I mostly hung around girls. Even though I had trouble making friends back then, I still had a few rare ones. One of them was a little boy, but that was way back in kindergarten when boys and girls don't think much of each other's genders. Average kids do that at that age, but I've always had a problem with dealing with big changes and sometimes I still do. As I grew up, I found ways to get through most of those life-altering changes, including puberty and other normal things that happen to people. My family members, friends, counselors, and teachers helped me learn more about the tough and confusing stuff I dealt with throughout my life; and they also gave me advice and sympathy whenever I needed it. I also sometimes have to repeatedly tell myself that, whatever myself or someone I know is going through, is normal and I'll get used to it over time.

T his chapter is about what people do for special needs people nowadays. This is something my teachers did for me at the Community Transition Program. I have a lot of social and job-related problems. One of my teachers came up with an idea called, "Tia's Social Stories." It's a folder to put examples of problems I struggle with and how I can solve them inside. This way, whenever I get confused, I can look at it and think, "Now I know what to do." Her teacher's assistants and I helped her with this. Here are some situations from the folder put in the exact order they were typed.

Social Story

Dealing with other people's opinion as opposed to my own

Chapter Eleven

when someone says: "Men are better than women at _____" (or other offensive things).

> I can say: "I disagree with you. There are plenty of women that are just as good as or better than men at _____" (or whatever offensive thing that was said).
>
> I say this in a calm and intelligent way. I can say: "I don't agree."
>
> I can walk away or remove myself from the conversation.
>
> If I can not remove myself from the situation then I can ignore the person and their conversation, write in a journal, or take deep breaths to calm down.

The next one helped me deal with customers on the first few weeks of volunteering at the Allenmore Hospital gift shop.

Tia's Script for Store

Customer hands you an item to buy.

You say: Is this all for you?

They say yes.

You say: Okay

You ring up the sale.

You say: That will be _____ please.

Customer gives you the money.

You say: Thank you.

Put the money in the register
and give back the change.

You say: Your change is _____ thank
you. Would you like your receipt?

During the first few weeks on the job, I was really overwhelmed by the new schedule. Even though I'm more flexible than I was a long time ago, it still takes me a little while to get used to new schedules. Plus, my people skills are still not that great. At least they are improving. I also still have a little trouble with dealing with mean people. That is why there's a "social story" about that. An example of one of my more recent "social stories" is one about how getting angry takes power away from you and gives it to whoever is picking on you at the moment. I had a hard time understanding that life lesson for a while, but I eventually got it.

In the state of Washington, there are political groups who help out people with all kinds of disabilities live normal lives. One of them is known as S.A.W. (Self Advocates of Washington). They are doing tons of amazing things! They occasionally come to the Community Transition Program and talk to my class about upcoming events involving special needs people. They also give us useful tips on how to advocate for ourselves. The one that I remember most specifically is how to speak in an assertive manner. They did a skit to illustrate that. It was about a schoolgirl boarding a bus full of kids who were poking fun at her. The first time, she acted passively and didn't stand up for herself. The second time, she acted aggressively by getting in one of the kid's faces; which I thought looked pretty funny. The third time showed the correct example, where the girl told the kids in a calm tone that she didn't appreciate the way they were treating her. The last try obviously worked for the character since she wasn't being extreme in any way. Somebody told me that sometimes people harass others anyway, even if they tell them they don't like it. That's unfortunately true, but at least the first person will come out looking like the better one if they're the assertive type.

Here is another great thing that S.A.W. has accomplished. Last year, they passed a law in

Olympia saying that the word "retarded" is illegal to write in documents concerning people with mental disabilities. Whoever uses that offensive word in a document will be fined. I'm still impressed with the fact that the law was passed. Unfortunately, a lot of people still use that word freely. There's nothing I can do about that except explain my disability to ignorant people who might insult me in that way. I also learned from my parents how to deal with people who don't care what I say. They said I should just walk away, because there's no use hanging around people who treat me unkindly. I agree completely. Sometimes it's really hard to ignore unnecessary comments, but whenever the situation isn't worth defending myself over, I try to blow it off anyway. It's even tough to do that at times, depending on what was said to or about me or about my kinds of people, but I eventually force myself to move on.

One time, I went to the capitol on a field trip for Advocacy Days, which is an event for discussing opportunities for disabled people. Before I went on the capitol trip, one of my teachers gave the class an assignment. She told her students to write down five issues that are important to them. These issues were to be discussed with the state legislators upon meeting them. This was a perfect opportunity to express at least some of my concerns. This is what I wrote down:

1. There should be more institutions for mentally disabled adults who can't live on their own or kids whose guardians can't handle them (I didn't write this part until now, but institutions should be a last resort if there's no other way to help those individuals with mental disabilities. They shouldn't be just left there and forgotten, ignored, or mistreated like people did in the old days, though).

2. There should be more job coaches/other kinds of help for disabled adults who can learn to live on their own.

3. There should be a budget for more after-school activities so that kids can stay out of trouble.

4. Bullying should be illegal or at least kids should get lectured about it (I didn't write this part down, but bullying causes serious psychological damage. That's why it's the number one cause of violence in schools. Take the 1990's Columbine High School shootings for example).

5. The laws against any kind of cruelty to people and animals should be harsher (i.e. child and animal abuse).

This list didn't get discussed right away, since the legislators were too busy at the time, but hopefully those "bill ideas" will be considered eventually. We did hand them to someone in that building. I learned that October is hopefully going to be Disability History Month! That is so exciting, since that is a big change for the world! Most average people used to disregard that kind of information a long time ago, since they felt that disabled people weren't important enough to discuss and learn about. That is so false! I was outraged when I first heard that. Here's one piece of information I learned from the letter I received about Disability History Month. Did you know that the phrase "ship of fools" comes from ships that transported mentally disabled people and abandoned them in port cities? I'll bet that happened hundreds of years ago. After I read that letter, I thought, *Why would people treat others that way? It makes no sense! They should've been better taken care of! Some of those people couldn't fend for themselves!*

E arlier in this autobiography, I wrote about myself having Obsessive Compulsive Disorder. I had to erase that because I don't have OCD. What I really have is just obsessive behavior. Not too long ago, I thought that obsessive behavior counts as Obsessive Compulsive Disorder. Mom corrected me and told me to look it up on a medical website. I did and I found out that she was right and I was wrong. I learned that obsessive behavior is only part of the disorder and not the whole thing. This is the definition I got off the internet. OCD is a psychological disorder that forces you to do certain rituals every day because you think that if you don't, bad things will happen. Take someone who locks the door three times before going out for example. They do that in order to avoid a break-in, even though they only need to lock the door once. I also learned that this disorder is related to Tourettes Syndrome. That, by the way, is hard to describe, but it basically means the same thing except it is slightly different. For example, a person with Tourettes Syndrome would either have a muscle tick or say random things in the middle of conversations which make the other people say, "Did he say that to me?"

I still have obsessive behavior and some of my other old habits. This is because, I forget not to do them every once in a while. I still have a little trouble with doing things like rubbing my hands and playing with my nose. I am a constant fidgeter. That is why my CTP teachers came up with a code to remind me to put my hands down or occupy myself with something else. All they have to do is say "hands" and I'll automatically put my hands down or behind my back. Or, I'll continue doing the activity I'm currently doing, like writing for example. At home or other places, I just need to start remembering to remind myself to stop whatever bad habit I'm doing because I look weird while doing them. Also, some of those habits—like slouching and touching my face—are bad for my health. I really need to work on not doing those things. I also need to try harder to control my obsessive behavior. Whenever I get fascinated with something, like guys for example, I tend to talk and think about it on a daily basis. After a while, it becomes annoying to whoever is listening to me. I agree with them on that, because this type of behavior can even get irritating to me as well. It's also tough for me to stop. I'm working on that though. I also still have problems with when it's appropriate to tell others what I'm thinking about certain subjects, like my sexuality, and when I'm better off keeping those types of things to myself. My parents taught me that some thoughts are okay to tell people I know, while other thoughts are better left unsaid.

I've also improved a little on dealing with people I don't like. I usually fixate on people who bother me, but for one whole week at Community Transition Program; I went without doing that. You want to know how I did it? I avoided certain people unless I absolutely needed to talk to them. Also, whenever I heard something I didn't like coming out of their mouths; I just kept my mouth shut and thought about something else. I figured out that this is what I should do from now on. That way, going to CTP was more bearable. It's not that I didn't like that class. The reason why I said ignoring certain people in that class would make it more bearable to go there is because some mornings I woke up thinking, "I don't want to go to CTP, but I have to. Besides, (name withheld and whoever hangs out with that person) might be absent today. Plus even if they're not, I've got three more months to tolerate them before they graduate! Then, I'll never see those people again!" Whenever I get annoyed with those types of people, I also remind myself to cool down and tell myself not to let them get to me.

Arguing and over-explaining are other problems I still face once in a while. I've been working on restraining myself from arguing lately, but there's still room for improvement. Old habits die hard, don't they? At least I'm not as bad as I was a few years ago. This is an example of how I still over-explain subjects. One night, I was watching *Oprah* with my parents. The topic being discussed on that particular episode was polygamy. While Oprah was interviewing some families who lived that kind of lifestyle, Mom said, "Why would anybody want to live like that?" I agreed with her, but I had to wait until the commercial break to share my opinion. During the advertisements, I said, "I think polygamy is morally wrong. I mean, what if the other people get jealous?"

"Then, they wouldn't get into that kind of relationship," Mom answered.

After that, I continued with, "Besides, doesn't God want it to be just one man and one woman and that's it?"

"That's what you believe," Mother replied.

"Well, I know that if that happened to me, I would feel like I've been cheated on! I only want one man," I said with a little bit of drama in my tone. Next, Dad tried to explain to me the fact that different people are raised differently. The example he used on me is the question of, what would I believe if my parents raised me to believe that it's okay for me to steal; as long as I get away with it. I answered, "I would probably think it was okay."

Dad replied, "Right, and that's how those families were raised." While watching that talk show, I learned a little bit more than I already knew about polygamy, but I still didn't quite get why some people do that stuff. My parents didn't either, and they didn't want to continue that discussion any further. This was because even though they were agreeing with me, I continued talking as though it wasn't already said. That's what Mom told me after she said I was fighting and I said, "No, I wasn't arguing. I was agreeing with you." She also asked me if, those people were hurting anyone by believing in something that I don't believe in. I said, "No."

She also told me, "We are a traditional family. We believe that when a man and a woman get together, they share intimacy that can't be shared with anyone else." She also told me that there are a lot of beliefs that our family doesn't understand; like why some people are gay for example. Even though I don't get that either, because I come from a long line of straight people and I'm straight as well, I think that being homosexual makes a little more sense than being polygamous. I was also appalled by the way those women were being treated in those polygamous communities described in that show.

Something I did in order to help me get over some of the issues I faced, other than going to my parents and family members, was to see the school psychologist. She was really nice, smart and trustworthy. She and I have known each other for a long time. She used to be one of my teachers in intermediate school. I still need to see a counselor on a regular basis and it is going good so far.

To change the subject, there are some relaxation techniques I use (elaborating on some things in chapter 7 with some new tips):

1. In order to de-stress myself at the end of a bad day, when I'm just not feeling tired (which isn't always stress-related); or just whenever I feel worried about some things in general, I sometimes go to bed with soft music playing. I also mentioned that I do this in order to calm myself down before a doctor's appointment. While listening to my Mp3 player at a low volume, my mind drifts off to a peaceful place. My favorite fantasy is picturing myself in the middle of a Zen garden, or some other Asian backdrop, taking in the beautiful scenery. Another

Chapter **Thirteen**

fantasy that helps me forget my troubles is me going on vacations to exotic places like Mexico and experiencing things I've always wanted to experience. One of those experiences is walking along the Great Wall of China or some other historical landmark I want to see some day and imagining what life must've been like centuries into the past. The music genres that work best for me are world, new age, and classical. I can't listen to anything loud like techno or rock during this situation, because it's less calming at night. Those are two genres that I only enjoy during the day. I can go on forever about the types of music I'm into, but sadly, I have to move on. Many other people apply this tip to their lives too … with their favorite music. Some of them even play it on a stereo system. Some people do that without headphones, which I find irritating. I would advise you to plug in headphones, so that whoever lives or is staying with you won't get disturbed by the noise.

2. If the above strategy doesn't work, I think about things that make me happy; like a story idea or something exciting that's going to happen in my future, until I fall asleep.

3. I love to take baths whenever I have a long or tough week. I also bathe at other times, just because it feels good and its part of good hygiene. The hot temperature of the water loosens my muscles. I like to listen to music while in the tub as well. Like I said, I use music for self healing or I just plain listen to it for fun. Any kind is usually okay in this situation, unless I'm in the mood for a certain type. When I get a chance, I also mix bubble bath or other scented chemicals in with the water. If I don't have bath beads or whatever, I either light scented candles or I go without scents. The scents are a small part of my relaxing atmosphere. Before I get into the tub, I only turn on the light that will be shining over my head while sitting in it. Different lighting can create different moods. It depends on where you are and what you're doing.

4. This is another thing I mentioned in chapter seven's list. Squeezing a stress ball works for me not only when I'm in a medical facility, but also during other stressful situations, or to stop myself from fidgeting whenever I have a ball with me.

5.   Whenever I'm writing one of my stories, it's like I go into my own little world. My mind goes off on adventures to whichever place and time period my books are set in. That's why a lot of people say that my imagery is very vivid and descriptive. I also get in touch with the characters I create, and get a little emotional whenever I put them through intense moments. Sometimes, I even have to pause and tell myself to get a hold of myself; since it's only a fiction story. This hobby makes me even more content than doing other things I like, like reading other people's books as one example. Like I mentioned earlier, I often dream about becoming a famous author. Hopefully, that will work out for me. I also like to listen to music while doing this activity, as I do during many activities. It keeps me focused on the task at hand, and it sometimes inspires my story ideas.

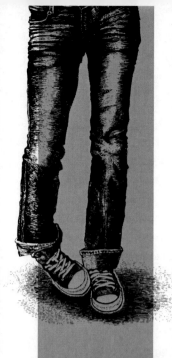

I learned from my teachers and parents to be assertive over the years. Yet, I still act passive-aggressively sometimes. I still have trouble with taking my anger out on people, even when it isn't their fault that I'm upset. I try not to, but at times it happens anyway. I'm slowly learning not to do that anymore. I also beat around the bush. For instance, one day I asked my mom if they ever did makeovers on guys on the show *What Not to Wear.* It's mostly a women's fashion show that teaches girls how to dress appropriately and look good for their ages and lifestyles. Mom said that they sometimes do makeovers for men on that show, but not very often since guys tend to look good just by doing very little to themselves. Girls tend to need more maintenance. I said,

Chapter Fourteen

"Well, I've never seen males on that show, and sometimes guys tend to let their facial hair grow out of whack."

Mom said, "So, then they'll shave it!" My mom then explained to me what the show was originally created for, and how it wouldn't teach women how to dress; if they showed men all the time.

Next, my mind went off on a tangent and suddenly this discussion turned into an argument about equality. I told Mom, "I like to watch guys on TV once in a while and most of the time, the television shows girls." Mom and Dad mentioned that I care too much about that. My parents said that it doesn't matter. They said, "A lot of people idolize women because they're more interesting to observe than men." My parents also told me there's more to women than men. That's true, but my point was since I'm a young woman, I prefer to look at men, because they're more attractive to me than women. No stereotype intended. Lately, I've been getting really irked about how someday I would like to see the world being fair. That includes people treating each other equally, whether they're males or females. Whenever I tell my family members this, it annoys them. I've told them where I stand on that issue thousands of times. I'm slowly learning that there are not always two sides to everything; no matter how badly I want there to be sometimes. Going off on tangents is something else I tend to do a lot whenever someone has a discussion with me. I do that to show them that I understand what they're saying to me. My parents taught me that the only thing I need to do sometimes is agree with the other person instead of going off on tangents. I also do that because I might want to talk about something someone mentioned in the middle of a conversation. But my parents are still teaching me not to over exaggerate, because if I do that every time I'm having a conversation with someone; we could be standing there all day. I'm learning that nobody wants to do that for more than a few hours or even minutes, depending on what the topic is.

I'm also working on not being passive-aggressive and not bringing up upsetting subjects at inappropriate times; like at the dinner table with my family, which unfortunately I do a lot. I'm also working on letting the little things go and keeping my thoughts to myself, unless I absolutely need to express them. For instance, if I'm being harassed or degraded; then it's perfectly fine to stand up for my rights. If I'm just listening to somebody else saying an opinion, in which I strongly disagree with; then I should stop listening to them. Dad told me that and he also told me if I see something I don't like on TV, then I should change the channel or turn it off.

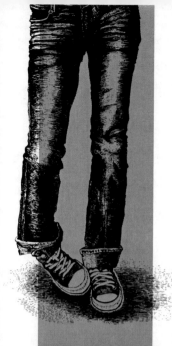

This is my "social story" about how getting angry gives the other person power over me:

When you get angry and react to someone, it gives them power over you and/or the situation.

Boy: "Girls should obey men at all times."

Tia (in an angry voice, fists up, shaking, angry face): "That's not true! Women should keep their rights because they earned them! Men should respect them! You're sexist!"

Boy now has the power, because you reacted so strongly, you gave him the power and he walks away laughing or saying something derogatory.

Or

You say (calm voice, hands folded or behind back, face

Chapter Fifteen

neutral/serious): "I disagree. Women are equal to men."

Boy: Laughs, makes more comments, etc.

Tia: Walks away, does not respond.

Tia has the power.

One of my teachers at Community Transition Program went over this with me shortly after a similar situation occurred. It's really tough for me not to get angry at someone who's purposely trying to upset me. I'm the type of person who wears their heart on their sleeve. If you don't know what that means, it means that I'm very open with my emotions and I show them all the time. Sometimes, I express them a little more than I should, which becomes a problem at times. It's especially hard to control myself when the really strong emotions like anger, sadness, infatuation, etc. come out. I'm learning to control that personality trait so that others won't be put off by it or take advantage of me while I'm in that vulnerable state. It's not that showing emotions is bad; it's just that people don't always need to be so extreme about that. This is another one of the many issues I'm learning to deal with ... and I'll probably face that challenge for the rest of my life. My family members told me that the only way to make these types of situations better is to improve on the ways I react to them. I've considered that for a very long time, but sometimes it's still a difficult idea for me to comprehend. Nobody said that life was easy, but that won't stop me from trying to learn as many social skills as I can.

I'd like to tell you some new things I learned recently. One weekend morning, Mom and I went to the Steilacoom Public Library to see a show about Japanese music and storytelling. I really enjoyed it, since I'm into that sort of thing. On top of that, I learned some interesting facts about Japan and traveling, which I never knew before. When the lady who was playing her koto (Japanese floor harp) took a short break in the middle of the show, she talked to the audience and answered some of their questions about the instrument and what the culture is like. She said she lived in Japan for twelve years and taught English at one of the schools there. Japanese people are required to learn that language when they're as young as sixth and seventh graders and keep on studying it through higher grades. I also learned that anyone who isn't Japanese is an outsider in that country. Unlike America, Japan isn't a "melting pot."

The performer said, "You can hardly see any-one of other races when you're at the airport." However, that isn't a racial issue. Even though it sounds like it. A lot of Japanese people are nice to foreigners or citizens that are different in actions or looks; they just consider them unusual, since they have a stereotypical view of what Americans are like. Japanese people tend to think Americans are outgoing and talkative, when only some of them are that way, while others are quieter and reserved like me. Sometimes I can be a little talk-ative, outgoing, and social; but mostly I just keep to myself and relax at home. These are just some of the things I learned at that event. Two other things I learned that really made me think are the old tradition that women are secondary to men is still around in that country. Plus, the fact that Jap-anese people stare at and gossip about anyone who is different from the majority of them, especially if they're not Japanese citizens. The treatment also differs if you have family in Japan, which I do not.

After the show, I asked the performer, "If I go to Japan as a tourist, how will they treat me, since I am a young woman, an American citizen, and I'm autistic?" I thought that those facts would be a triple whammy for me if I ever planned on going there some day. I was unsure about being able to handle the things the locals would say about or to me.

She said, "People would stare at you since you're tall, have blonde hair, etc." I told her that I heard that most (but not all) Asians are short, have black hair, etc. She agreed with me. After Mom told her a little bit about my Autism, she told me, "Japanese people are definitely going to stare at you and talk about you. It will probably make you feel self-conscious and you have to decide whether you're going to be angry, uncomfortable, or okay with that. Also, when you travel to a different country, don't go there with the attitude that you're going to change the country. You go there accepting their cultures the way they are." She also said that I look like a shy person and I told her that was true and it takes some time for me to warm up to new people.

I told my mom as we were leaving, "I don't know if I can handle the fact that the old Japanese tradition of women being secondary to men is still around." I didn't need to explain myself any further, and she told me the same thing as that lady told me. I then said, "I'm going to have to learn to deal with that since I still think it would be nice to visit there some day."

My mom's reply was, "Yeah, it would be cool to visit there, but it doesn't sound like a good place for you to live."

I agreed with her and then added, "I don't know how she did it for twelve years."

Mom said, "Well, they accepted her a little more because she provided a service for them, since they're required to learn English. They probably won't treat you the same as her because you wouldn't provide any services for them."

I stated, "I would just be there to have a good time and explore the country." She agreed with that and that's where the conversation ended.

My thoughts about the show I saw at the Steilacoom Public Library, sort of made me think of a story I heard at CTP. One of my teacher's friends went to China once. He or she said that they don't accommodate special needs people there. They don't even have wheelchairs. They just lock them all up in institutions. This practice has to do with the "one-child-per-household" laws. China's communist government came up with those laws to control the population. However, most couples do not want their child to be disabled; and when that happens, their parents disown them. That is very awful. Everybody needs to be loved, whether they are disabled or not. After hearing those things, I felt so sad and discouraged that I went home at the end of the day and cried . China is the inspiration for most of my stories. Most aspects of the Chinese culture are really beautiful, including the traditional music, the artwork, the traditional clothing, etc. Even the ideal man in most of my dreams has an Asian look to him, even though I think there are good-looking men in every race. Another reason why those unfortunate facts brought me to tears is because I always feel sorry for those who are less fortunate. At the same time, hearing bad news like people living in foreign countries where they have no freedom to believe in whatever they want; makes me feel lucky to be an American girl with those types of freedoms. I also believe that it's morally wrong and unfair to persecute people just because of their disability, or religious affiliation. Hopefully, the human rights issues will be resolved in China someday. I would still like to go there and see the good things about that country.

This is the story about when I was diagnosed with Autism. I talked to my mother and father about this and they said it happened when I was five. My early teachers told my folks that they noticed I acted very differently compared to the other children. I was very slow in developing my gross-motor skills and my social skills. An example of how my gross-motor skills used to be is when I ran; I would fling my arms and legs around wildly while other kids ran straight. As I grew up, my gross-motor skills improved dramatically. I also developed way better social skills. When I was much too young to remember a lot of things, my teachers said that instead of playing with the other kids; I would rather sit in the corner, play with my fingers, and stare

Chapter Sixteen

at the wall. They thought something was wrong with me and so did my parents. Remember, at that time, many people didn't know much about Autism. So, my parents took me to the University of Washington to run some tests to see if there was anything abnormal about me. After a couple weeks, nobody could figure out what my issue was. Two years later, I went to get re-tested at the same place. The child psychologists who worked there diagnosed me with Autism, which surprised and probably shocked everybody I knew.

I also want to add some comments about a book on Autism I recently read. I hope people won't mistake this paragraph for infringing on copyright laws. I just want to say a few things about a book I learned a lot from and could relate to. Recently I finished reading Temple Grandin's book, "Emergence." It was about her life as an autistic person and how she sort of "recovered" from it. The two facts I remember the most from her book were, that getting squeezed can calm most autistics. Although I personally probably would not have liked the feeling of the "human cattle chute" that she invented. Also, I learned that Autism was discovered by Dr. Leo Kanner in 1943; when he did studies on some little boys who had it. It used to be called Kanner's Syndrome, and then the name got changed over time. That was an interesting tidbit about the origin, even though nobody still knows the cause of Autism. So, old movies about people with Autism are no longer the oldest historical proof of that disability I've heard of; and I'll probably learn a lot more about disability history in the future. What also made Temple's book interesting is that, she went through some of the same issues I did. We both obsess a lot, although my obsessions are different than hers. We also both had sudden outbursts throughout our lives. There is a place where I like to escape to a lot, kind of like when she used to climb into the unfinished level of her high school. That comfortable place for me is my room. It is a lot less thrilling to go there, but this is a place where I can relax whenever I get stressed out; and think about life. It is also a suitable place to just hang out in whenever I am at home. Also, the stories of when we went through puberty were similar; only I did not go up to one of the boys and say what she said to him. (By the way, that part made me blush and giggle a little as well as think, "I remember when I first felt that way.") I can also relate to the fact that she got ostracized for having

The Disregarded Child

109

a mental disability most of the time. Anyone who is different from "everybody else" can probably relate to that. She and I also agree on feminism in a way, even though I personally would like to get married and all that entails. While there may still be sexist people out there, there are still men who treat women with respect and see them as equal members of society. It would be kind of cool to meet her someday, or someone like her. We might become good friends.

In 2009, I graduated from CTP early. I was supposed to graduate after I turned 21, but I proved to my teachers that I was independent and mature enough to go out into the real world. As long as I can get a little help every now and then, I should be fine; once I get the hang of things. Even though I have managed to succeed in school, I still have some things to work on in my personal life. Social cues are still difficult for me to comprehend sometimes, and I think that will continue to affect me. I also have to be reminded of some of the things I have learned at times. I also know my limits, like not being able to drive for example. I tried taking driving lessons from my dad a couple times at his auto wrecking shop, when I was in my late teens. At first, I felt excited to be learning how to drive since it's a right of passage for most people. But then after I tried it, it became an experience which was a little scary. I kept on crashing into other cars in the wrecking yard. Thank God there were no injuries, but that experience made me think of the horrible things that would have happened; if I had been out on the road. Not to be negative or anything, but that is when I realized that; I can never take Driver's Ed. Not only that, but there are also way too many rules of the road for me to memorize all at once; and I cannot concentrate on more than a couple things at a time. When people are on the road, they have to pay attention to several things at once; and they also have to know exactly what the other drivers around them are doing. I often have a hard time putting myself in other's shoes, so that would impair me while driving as well as not being very good at multi-tasking. I prefer taking special buses or other means of public transportation, and asking other people I know for rides. I have gone over many hurdles in life, and will continue to. But, no matter what kinds of challenges I have faced and will face; I will still try my best to live life to the fullest and will continue to learn about life, as well as writing other books, which I pray that you will love just as much as this story.